Adele's Big Bird, page 22; Cranberry-Orange Relish, page 48;
Orange-Kissed Sweet Potatoes, page 42; Steamed Green Beans

Cherry-Berry Pie, page 79

HOME
FOR THE HOLIDAYS
COOKBOOK

Library of Congress Catalog Card Number: 95-71317
ISBN: 0-8487-1518-7
Manufactured in the United States of America
First Printing 1995

Editor-in-Chief: Nancy Fitzpatrick Wyatt
Senior Editor, Editorial Services: Olivia Kindig Wells
Art Director: James Boone

Home for the Holidays

Senior Foods Editor: Susan Carlisle Payne
Copy Editor: Keri Bradford Anderson
Editorial Assistants: Alison Rich Lewis, Susan Hernandez
Designer: Eleanor Cameron
Production and Distribution Director: Phillip Lee
Associate Production Manager: Theresa L. Beste
Production Assistant: Marianne Jordan Wilson

To order more copies of HOME FOR THE HOLIDAYS COOKBOOK
write to Oxmoor House, P.O. Box 2463, Birmingham, AL 35201

❧ Contents ❧

This book is dedicated to our mothers, who taught us everything about saying "thank you" on command, overeating, and the culinary miracle of salt.

"There she is. Oh, my God—she looks so skinny."

✣ Introduction ✣

W e all do it. We fend for our lives in crowded airports, sit through endless family button-pushing, stuff ourselves and our birds with god knows what, and wonder . . . why. Sure, there's the Pilgrim Thing, that tired Thanksgiving story peppered with corn husks, buckle hats, and the gift of giving. Personally, I don't buy it. Someone invented this twisted yearly ritual simply, and most profoundly, to torture our psyches.

We are lured by the comfort of delicious yet disgusting food ("Can you prove that I actually ate that?"), guilt-tripped by the fantasy of familial love ("Why do I sometimes feel like I'm stuck in an elevator with aliens?"), jettisoned back to our basest behaviors, and put face to face, cheek to cheek with our own too often neurotic humanity.

Take Jello salad, for example. (We never make it, but I pray some unsuspecting guest will bring it.) You know, the green kind tossed with mint-colored cubes all spiked with Cool Whip and canned pineapple.

How come the rest of the year I confine my identity to the likeness of halibut sashimi, multivitamins, and yoga class, only to find myself salivating over that shaky green mass on the fourth Thursday of each November?

Don't get me wrong, now. We Fosters are a pretty sophisticated bunch when it comes to the fated feast. We pretty much serve the same poster meal that my mother always cooked. Since my mother has happily vowed to never cook again, she has the supreme position of ordering the sexy-yet-store-bought hors d'oeuvres like smoked salmon, pâté, or caviar. This way she gets to roll her eyes and mumble, "I told you not to take the cheesecloth off," if any portion of the meal doesn't live up to her personal mythology. But we wouldn't have it any other way. We all enjoy cooking and seem to get through it without being paralyzed by any inherited perfection complex.

My sister, Connie, is the great chef of the family, even though she always forgets one item in the oven. And because of my eternal "baby" position in the family, I get to make the Foster orange cups, a huge honor, if you hadn't guessed it already. They are the most impressive and easiest-to-make dish of the day. Not only do they travel well in Tupperware, they also contain liberal amounts of alcohol AND sugar.

The Fosters' Famous Thanksgiving Orange Cups

6   navel oranges, cut in half crosswise
7   or 8 yams or sweet potatoes, peeled
1   stick butter
Grand Marnier liqueur to taste
Few shakes ground cloves
Few shakes ground nutmeg
Salt and pepper to taste
12 pecans for garnish

Scoop out all the orange pulp, and squeeze the juice. Save the juice but not the pulp. Boil potatoes until soft and ready to mash. Strain potatoes, add butter, and mash. Add juice and liqueur to taste. Mix with electric beater until consistency is of soft mashed potatoes. Add cloves, nutmeg, salt, and pepper. You can even add a little brown sugar if it tastes too tart. Scoop the mixture into orange cups. Dot the top with a pecan. Orange cups can be made a couple of days early. Just keep them refrigerated. When ready to serve, just heat in a baking dish at 325° until warmed. Yield: 12 servings.

Since I crave popularity in my family, this recipe's right up my alley. When the family drama starts flying, at least those silly oranges affirm two facts: Nothing changes, and it probably won't kill you anyway. Thanksgiving is intimate, and that's not always good news.

Honestly, my favorite part of Thanksgiving is the week that follows. After I've either been loaded down (or done some loading down) with serious leftovers, my friends, and sometimes returning family, start dropping by for spontaneous dinners. There's a lot of laughing and microwave beeps. Some people only go for the stuffing. Others opt for the whole nine yards.

But there we all are in jogging pants cracking jokes, eating the same meal that drove everybody crazy a few days before. Only this time, the pressure's off. We don't have to hold hands in some Go-Figure tradition of buckle hats and the gift of giving. We're just family— and mostly because we choose to be.

I guess it just goes to show that no matter how hard you try, things taste better when they're a few days old and wrapped in your very own plastic.

Jodie Foster

Recipe Symbols

FIT FOR FEASTING indicates extravagant recipes like Henry and Adele make—the ones you hate to love.

LEAN & MEAN represents lighter nouvelle fare straight from Joanne's kitchen.

VERY VEGETARIAN connotes healthy meatless marvels that are "Classically Claudia."

On Your Mark ... Get Set
❖ appetizers & beverages ❖

This course is sort of like Babe Ruth pointing to the fence before hitting another home run. You make a commitment right off the bat to outdo yourself.

Shrimpy Artichoke Dip

2   (14-ounce) cans artichoke hearts, drained and chopped
2   cups grated Parmesan cheese
2   cups mayonnaise
2   (6-ounce) packages frozen crabmeat with shrimp, thawed,
      drained, and flaked
½   cup Italian-seasoned breadcrumbs

Combine first 4 ingredients, mixing well. Spoon into a greased 1½-quart baking dish. Top with breadcrumbs. Bake at 325° for 15 to 20 minutes. Serve with crackers. Yield: 12 servings.

Reindeer Fodder Mix

6   cups mini-pretzels
6   cups goldfish-shaped crackers
3   cups bite-size Cheddar cheese crackers
3   cups crispy rice cereal squares
½   cup butter or margarine, melted
2   tablespoons Worcestershire sauce
1½ teaspoons seasoning salt

Combine first 4 ingredients. Combine butter, Worcestershire sauce, and seasoning salt; pour over pretzel mixture, tossing to coat. Spread mixture in a broiler pan. Bake at 250° for 30 minutes, stirring twice. Cool; store in airtight container. Yield: 4½ quarts.

Four-Cheese Pâté

1   *(8-ounce) package cream cheese, softened*
2   *tablespoons milk*
2   *tablespoons sour cream*
¾   *cup chopped pecans, toasted*
2   *(8-ounce) packages cream cheese, softened*
1   *(4½-ounce) package Camembert cheese, softened*
1   *(4-ounce) package crumbled blue cheese, softened*
1   *cup (4 ounces) shredded Swiss cheese, softened*

Line a 9-inch pieplate with plastic wrap. Combine first 3 ingredients; beat at medium speed of an electric mixer until smooth. Spread into pieplate; sprinkle with pecans.

Combine remaining cream cheese, Camembert cheese (including rind), blue cheese, and Swiss cheese in a mixing bowl; beat at medium speed until smooth. Spoon into pieplate, and spread to edge. Cover and chill up to 1 week.

To serve, invert pâté onto a serving plate; carefully peel away plastic wrap. Serve with red and green apple wedges. Yield: 4½ cups.

"I can see your roots, Claudia."

Whirlwind Pastries

1   large green pepper
1   large sweet red pepper
2   tablespoons sesame seeds, toasted
2   cups all-purpose flour
1   cup grated Parmesan cheese
½   teaspoon ground red pepper
¾   cup butter
⅓   cup plus 1 tablespoon water

Cut peppers in half; discard seeds and membranes. Place pepper halves, skin side up, on a foil-lined baking sheet; flatten with palm of hand.

Broil peppers 3 inches from heat (with electric door partially opened) 5 minutes or until blackened and charred. Place peppers in a heavy-duty, zip-top plastic bag; seal bag, and let stand 15 minutes to loosen skins. Peel and discard skins. Chop peppers finely.

Combine chopped pepper and sesame seeds; set aside. Combine flour, cheese, and ground red pepper; cut in butter with a pastry blender until mixture is crumbly. Sprinkle water evenly over surface; stir with a fork until dry ingredients are moistened. Shape into 4 balls; cover and chill.

Roll one ball of dough into a 10- x 7-inch rectangle on a lightly floured surface; spread dough evenly with one-fourth of pepper mixture. Roll dough, jellyroll fashion, beginning with long end. Seal edges of dough; wrap roll in wax paper, and chill at least 2 hours. Repeat procedure with remaining dough and pepper mixture.

Cut rolls into ¼-inch slices. Place on lightly greased baking sheets; bake at 400° for 11 to 12 minutes or until edges are lightly browned. Cool 1 minute on baking sheets; transfer to wire racks, and let cool completely. Yield: 12 dozen.

Note: Adele makes these as early as Halloween and freezes the rolls in an airtight container. Then she thaws them just a little and bakes them by the recipe.

Snockered 'Nog

6	egg yolks
¾	cup sugar
1	tablespoon vanilla extract
¼	teaspoon freshly grated nutmeg
4	cups milk
1	(12-ounce) can evaporated milk
1	(14-ounce) can sweetened condensed milk
½	cup dark rum
½	cup brandy

Sweetened whipped cream
Freshly grated nutmeg

Beat egg yolks at medium speed of an electric mixer until thick and pale; gradually beat in sugar, vanilla, and ¼ teaspoon nutmeg.

Place 4 cups milk in a large saucepan over medium-low heat. Gradually add yolk mixture; cook, stirring constantly with a wire whisk, until mixture reaches 160°. Remove from heat; let cool. Stir in evaporated milk, sweetened condensed milk, rum, and brandy. Cover and chill.

When ready to serve, top each serving with whipped cream, and sprinkle with freshly grated nutmeg. Yield: 9 quarts.

Cheesy Stuffed Celery

½   (8-ounce) package Neufchâtel cheese, softened
½   cup (2 ounces) shredded 40% less-fat Cheddar cheese
¼   cup plain nonfat yogurt
2   tablespoons chopped pecans
2   tablespoons diced pimiento
½   teaspoon dry mustard
¼   teaspoon hot sauce
⅛   teaspoon pepper
30   (3-inch) celery sticks
Paprika

Combine first 3 ingredients; stir well. Add pecans and next 4 ingredients; stir gently.

Spoon cheese mixture evenly into celery sticks; sprinkle with paprika. Cover and chill at least 30 minutes. Yield: 2½ dozen (22 calories each).

"Float. Just float."

Appetizer Broccoli Soup

Vegetable cooking spray
1   cup chopped onion
6   cups fresh chopped broccoli
²⁄₃   cup thinly sliced carrot
2   (10½-ounce) cans ready-to-serve, no-salt-added chicken
       broth
1   cup water
¾   teaspoon salt
½   teaspoon pepper
½   teaspoon dried thyme
1¼ cups skim milk
Garnish: carrot curls

Coat a Dutch oven with cooking spray; place over medium
heat until hot. Add onion, and cook, stirring constantly, until
tender. Stir in broccoli, carrot, chicken broth, water, salt,
pepper, and thyme. Bring to a boil; cover, reduce heat, and
simmer 15 minutes or until vegetables are tender. Remove
from heat; let cool slightly.

   Place half of broccoli mixture in container of an electric
blender; cover and process until smooth, stopping once to
scrape down sides. Repeat procedure with remaining broccoli
mixture. Return to Dutch oven; stir in milk, and cook over
medium heat until thoroughly heated. Spoon into serving
bowls, and garnish, if desired. Yield: 8 cups (56 calories per
1-cup serving).

Note: Soup can be made up to 2 days ahead and chilled.
Heat thoroughly before serving.

Dad's Fuzzy Navel

1½ cups skim milk
1½ cups frozen unsweetened sliced peaches
1 (6-ounce) can frozen orange juice concentrate, thawed and
    undiluted
12 ice cubes
2 tablespoons peach schnapps
1 (8-ounce) carton plain nonfat yogurt

Combine first 5 ingredients in container of an electric blender;
cover and process until smooth. Add yogurt, and process just
until blended. Pour into glasses, and serve immediately. Yield:
5 cups (136 calories per 1-cup serving).

Berry-Good Cider

2 cups sparkling apple cider, chilled
1½ cups cranberry juice cocktail, chilled
¾ cup lemon-lime flavored sparkling water, chilled
Garnishes: cranberries and lime slices

Combine first 3 ingredients in a pitcher; stir well. Pour into
glasses; garnish each with a cranberry and a lime slice, if
desired. Serve immediately. Yield: 4 cups (76 calories per
⅔-cup serving).

Berry-Good Cider, facing page

Adele's Big Bird, page 22

Give Your Family the Bird

❖ entrées ❖

The holiday bird just wouldn't be nearly
as delicious unless its golden aroma mixed with
your great aunt's perfume and clashed with
mother's wallpaper. Life is funny like that.

Adele's Big Bird

Vegetable cooking spray
1   *(10- to 12-pound) turkey*
2   *teaspoons salt*
2   *teaspoons lemon-pepper seasoning*
1   *medium onion, quartered*
Fresh parsley sprigs
2   *teaspoons dried rosemary, divided*
1   *large onion, sliced*
1   *carrot, sliced*
1   *celery stalk, sliced*
1½ *cups chicken broth*
1   *cup dry white wine*
½   *cup brandy or Cognac*
½   *cup tomato juice*
¼   *cup cornstarch*
⅓   *cup whipping cream*
1   *teaspoon browning-and-seasoning sauce*

Line a large roasting pan with heavy-duty aluminum foil, leaving a 3-inch overhang on all sides. Spray foil with cooking spray. Set aside. Remove giblets and neck from turkey; set aside. Rinse turkey; pat dry.

Sprinkle cavities with salt and lemon-pepper seasoning. Place onion quarters in neck cavity. Place several parsley sprigs and 1 teaspoon rosemary into other cavity. Tie ends of legs to tail with cord, or tuck them under flap of skin around tail. Lift wingtips up and over back; tuck under turkey.

Place turkey in prepared pan, breast side up; arrange giblets, sliced onion, carrot, and celery around turkey. Sprinkle giblets and vegetables with remaining 1 teaspoon rosemary.

Combine chicken broth and next 3 ingredients in a medium saucepan; cook until thoroughly heated. Pour mixture over turkey. Cover with a sheet of heavy-duty aluminum foil, without letting foil touch turkey. Fold edges of foil together, and crimp to form an airtight seal.

Bake at 425° for 1½ hours on lowest rack in oven. Cut a lengthwise slit in top of foil; fold sides of foil back. Insert meat thermometer into meaty portion of thigh, making sure it does not touch bone. Cut cord or band of skin holding the drumstick ends to tail. Reduce heat to 400°; bake 1 hour or until meat thermometer registers 180°. (Do not baste.) Turkey is done when drumsticks are easy to move up and down.

Pour drippings through a wire-mesh strainer into a medium saucepan, discarding giblets and vegetables. Combine cornstarch and whipping cream; gradually stir into drippings. Bring mixture to a boil, stirring constantly; boil 1 minute, stirring constantly. Remove from heat; stir in browning-and-seasoning sauce. Serve gravy with turkey. Yield: 12 to 14 servings.

"I was told he wouldn't be here, Joanne. So I didn't prepare myself. I have to sit here and prepare myself."

A Real Stuffed Turkey

1 (12-ounce) package bacon, chopped
1 cup chopped onion
3 (10-ounce) packages frozen chopped spinach, thawed and
    well drained
2 eggs, lightly beaten
1 cup ricotta cheese
¾ teaspoon garlic salt
¾ teaspoon dried oregano
½ teaspoon freshly ground pepper
1 (5- to 6-pound) bone-in turkey breast
⅓ cup butter or margarine, melted

Cook bacon in a large skillet until crisp; drain well. Pour off all but ¼ cup drippings; add onion to drippings in skillet, and cook, stirring constantly, until tender. Stir in spinach; cook, uncovered, 5 minutes, stirring frequently. Cool slightly.

Combine eggs and cheese; blend well. Stir in spinach mixture, reserved bacon, garlic salt, oregano, and pepper.

Remove skin and bone from turkey breast. Place turkey, boned side up, on heavy-duty plastic wrap. Starting from center, cut horizontally through thickest portion of each side of breast almost to, but not through, outer edges. Flip cut pieces over to enlarge breast. Cover turkey with heavy-duty plastic wrap; flatten to an even thickness, using a meat mallet or rolling pin. (Place loose pieces of turkey over thinner portions.)

Spread spinach mixture over turkey breast to within 2 inches of edges. Roll up, jellyroll fashion, starting with short side. Close and secure ends with wooden picks. Tie securely at 2-inch intervals with heavy string. Place seam side down on a greased rack in a roasting pan. Brush butter evenly over turkey roll. Bake, uncovered, at 325° for 2 hours, brushing occasionally with butter. Let stand 15 minutes. Remove strings; cut turkey roll into slices. Yield: 10 to 12 servings.

Herb Butter-Basted Turkey Breast

½	cup butter or margarine
¼	cup lemon juice
2	tablespoons minced green onions
2	tablespoons soy sauce
1	teaspoon dried sage, crushed
1	teaspoon dried thyme
1	teaspoon dried marjoram
½	teaspoon salt
¼	teaspoon pepper
1	(5- to 5½-pound) bone-in turkey breast

Combine all ingredients except turkey in a saucepan; bring to a boil. Remove from heat; set aside.

Place turkey breast, skin side up, in a lightly oiled 13- x 9- x 2-inch pan; baste with butter mixture. Cover turkey with foil. Insert meat thermometer through foil into thickest portion of breast, making sure it does not touch bone. Enlarge opening in foil so thermometer does not touch foil. Bake at 325° for 2 hours or until thermometer registers 170°, basting often with butter mixture. Transfer turkey to serving platter. Yield: 10 to 12 servings.

Larson Family Jewels

1	(16-rib) crown roast of pork (8 to 9 pounds)
1	teaspoon salt, divided
¼	teaspoon pepper, divided
⅓	cup chopped onion
2	tablespoons butter or margarine, melted
1	cup uncooked instant rice
1¼ cups water
¼	teaspoon poultry seasoning
¾	cup chopped dried prunes
⅓	cup chopped dried apricots

Garnishes: kumquats and watercress

Season roast with ½ teaspoon salt and ⅛ teaspoon pepper; place roast, bone ends up, on greased rack in a shallow roasting pan. Insert meat thermometer, making sure it does not touch fat or bone. Bake roast at 325° for 1½ hours.

Cook onion in butter in a large skillet over medium heat, stirring constantly, until tender. Add rice, water, ½ teaspoon salt, ⅛ teaspoon pepper, and poultry seasoning to onion; stir well. Bring rice mixture to a boil; remove from heat. Cover tightly, and let stand 10 minutes. Stir in prunes and apricots.

Remove pork roast from oven; fill center of roast with rice mixture. Cover stuffing and exposed ends of ribs with aluminum foil. Bake at 325° for 2½ hours or until meat thermometer registers 160°. Remove from oven, and place on a serving platter. Garnish bone tips with kumquats, if desired. Garnish platter with watercress, if desired. Yield: 8 to 12 servings.

Note: Cooking time equals 25 to 30 minutes per pound and can be used to determine cooking time for smaller roasts.

Orange-Glazed Ham

1   (7- to 8-pound) smoked, fully cooked ham half
1   cup orange juice
1   cup ginger ale
½   cup firmly packed brown sugar
2   tablespoons vegetable oil
1   tablespoon white vinegar
2   teaspoons dry mustard
½   teaspoon ground ginger
¼   teaspoon ground cloves

Remove skin from ham; trim fat to ¼- to ⅛-inch thickness. Place ham in a large heavy-duty, zip-top plastic bag.

Combine orange juice and remaining ingredients; pour 2 cups mixture over ham. Seal bag, and place in a shallow pan or dish; marinate 8 hours, turning occasionally. Cover and chill remaining orange juice mixture.

Remove ham from marinade, discarding marinade. Place ham, fat side up, on a greased rack in a shallow roasting pan; insert meat thermometer, making sure it does not touch fat or bone. Bake at 325° for 2 to 2½ hours or until meat thermometer registers 140°, basting with reserved orange juice mixture every 20 minutes. (If ham starts to darken too much, cover loosely with aluminum foil after 1 hour.) Yield: 14 servings.

Beef Tenderloin with Peppercorns

1   (4- to 6-pound) beef tenderloin, trimmed
3   tablespoons Dijon mustard
1   tablespoon dried sage
1½ tablespoons green peppercorns, drained
1½ tablespoons black peppercorns, ground and divided
1½ tablespoons white peppercorns, ground and divided
2   tablespoons butter, softened

Trim excess fat from tenderloin. Cut tenderloin lengthwise down center, cutting to, but not through, bottom. Open tenderloin out flat. Place heavy-duty plastic wrap on tenderloin; pound meat to flatten slightly. Remove wrap; spread mustard evenly on meat. Sprinkle evenly with sage, green peppercorns, and ½ tablespoon each of black and white ground peppercorns.

Fold tenderloin back over, and tie securely with heavy string at 3-inch intervals. Spread softened butter over outside, and sprinkle with remaining ground peppercorns.

Place tenderloin on a lightly greased rack in a roasting pan; insert meat thermometer into thickest portion of tenderloin. Bake at 425° for 30 to 45 minutes or until meat thermometer registers 145° (medium-rare) or 160° (medium). Let stand 10 minutes before slicing. Yield: 10 to 12 servings.

Adele's Famous Meat Loaf

1½ pounds ground beef
2   (8-ounce) cans tomato sauce, divided
1   cup soft breadcrumbs
2   large eggs, lightly beaten
2   tablespoons dried onion flakes
¾   teaspoon salt
¼   teaspoon pepper
2   teaspoons dried parsley flakes
1   teaspoon Worcestershire sauce

Combine ground beef, ½ cup tomato sauce, and next 5 ingredients; mix well. Shape meat mixture into a loaf. Place on lightly greased rack in a broiler pan. Bake at 350° for 1 hour.

    Combine remaining tomato sauce, parsley, and Worcestershire sauce; stir well. Pour over meat loaf, and bake an additional 5 minutes. Yield: 6 servings.

Henry's Hurry-up Meat Loaves:
Shape meat mixture into 6 individual loaves; place on lightly greased rack in a broiler pan. Bake at 450° for 25 minutes or to desired degree of doneness. Add topping as directed for whole meat loaf.

Very Vegetable Paella

½   cup boiling water
¼   teaspoon threads of saffron
Vegetable cooking spray
1   teaspoon olive oil
2   tablespoons minced garlic
¾   cup sliced green onions
¾   cup diced sweet red pepper
1   (9-ounce) package frozen artichoke hearts, thawed and
        quartered
3   cups canned vegetable broth, undiluted
1½ cups long-grain brown rice, uncooked
1   cup no-salt-added tomatoes, drained and chopped
2   teaspoons Hungarian sweet paprika
1   (15-ounce) can cannellini beans, drained
1   cup thinly sliced arugula
¾   cup frozen English peas, thawed
½   cup freshly grated Parmesan cheese
½   teaspoon freshly ground pepper

Combine boiling water and saffron; cover and let stand 10
minutes. Coat a large saucepan with cooking spray; add olive
oil. Place over medium-high heat until hot. Add garlic, and
cook, stirring constantly, 1 minute. Add green onions, red pepper, and artichoke hearts; cook, stirring constantly, 5 minutes.

   Stir in saffron water, broth, rice, tomatoes, and paprika.
Bring to a boil; cover, reduce heat, and cook 15 minutes. Stir
in beans, arugula, and peas; cover and cook 15 minutes or
until liquid is absorbed and rice is tender. Remove from heat;
let stand 5 minutes. Spoon into a serving bowl; sprinkle with
cheese and pepper. Yield: 6 servings (347 calories per serving).

Joanne's
Apricot-Glazed Ham

1   (8½-pound) smoked, reduced-sodium, fully cooked ham half
About 40 whole cloves
Vegetable cooking spray
1   (10-ounce) jar no-sugar-added apricot spread
¾   cup unsweetened orange juice
1   tablespoon Dijon mustard
1½   teaspoons grated fresh ginger
¾   teaspoon hot sauce

Remove skin from ham; trim fat. Make shallow cuts in a diamond pattern on outside of ham, and insert cloves in center of diamonds. Place ham on a rack coated with cooking spray; place rack in a shallow roasting pan. Insert meat thermometer, making sure it does not touch fat or bone. Bake at 325° for 1 hour.

Combine apricot spread and remaining ingredients; set aside 1 cup mixture. Brush ham lightly with remaining mixture, and cover with aluminum foil. Bake at 325° for 2 hours or until meat thermometer registers 140°, basting with apricot mixture every 30 minutes.

Warm 1 cup reserved apricot mixture; serve with ham. Yield: 20 servings (190 calories per 3-ounce serving).

Peppered Beef Surprise Packages

1   cup chopped zucchini
1   cup chopped fresh mushrooms
½   cup finely chopped onion
1   clove garlic, minced
¼   teaspoon salt
Butter-flavored vegetable cooking spray
8   (4-ounce) beef tenderloin steaks
2   tablespoons cracked pepper
16 sheets commercial frozen phyllo pastry, thawed
Garnishes: tomato rosette and fresh parsley

Cook first 5 ingredients in a nonstick skillet coated with cooking spray over medium-high heat until tender. Remove from heat, and set aside.

Sprinkle both sides of steaks with pepper; set aside. Coat a nonstick skillet with cooking spray; place over high heat until hot. Add steaks, and cook 1½ minutes on each side. Remove from skillet; set aside.

Place 1 sheet phyllo on a towel. (Keep remaining phyllo covered.) Coat phyllo sheet with cooking spray. Fold in half lengthwise, and place 1 steak 3 inches from end. Spoon 2 tablespoons vegetable mixture onto steak, and fold short end of phyllo over stuffing. Fold sides of pastry over steak, and roll up.

Place a second sheet of phyllo on a towel; cut into a 12-inch square, and coat with cooking spray. Place wrapped steak, vegetable side up, in center. Bring corners of square to the middle, gently pressing together in center. Pull ends up and out to resemble a package. Coat bundle with cooking spray; place on a baking sheet coated with cooking spray. Repeat procedure with remaining steaks, phyllo, and vegetable mixture.

Bake at 400° for 17 minutes for medium-rare or 20 minutes for medium. Serve immediately. Garnish, if desired. Yield: 8 servings (301 calories per serving).

Apple-Glazed Pork Roast

1   (2-pound) rolled boneless pork loin roast
Vegetable cooking spray
¼   cup apple jelly, melted
2   tablespoons Dijon mustard
½   teaspoon garlic powder

Trim fat from roast; place roast on a rack coated with cooking spray. Place rack in a shallow roasting pan.

Combine jelly, mustard, and garlic powder; brush over roast. Insert meat thermometer into thickest portion of roast. Bake at 325° for 1 hour and 55 minutes or until meat thermometer registers 160°, basting frequently with jelly mixture. Let stand 10 minutes before slicing. Yield: 8 servings (about 236 calories per 3-ounce serving).

Note: Check out the Topless Pork Sandwiches on page 105 when you get tired of eating these leftovers cold.

Glorious Nutri-Bird

1   (12-pound) turkey
6   fresh thyme sprigs, divided
4   fresh rosemary sprigs, divided
4   fresh sage sprigs, divided
½   teaspoon poultry seasoning
¼   teaspoon salt
¼   teaspoon pepper
1   medium onion, quartered
2   stalks celery, quartered
Vegetable cooking spray
Garnishes: fresh rosemary, sage, and thyme sprigs

Remove and discard giblets and neck from turkey. Rinse turkey; pat dry. Trim excess fat. Starting at neck cavity, loosen skin from breasts and drumsticks by inserting one hand, palm side down. Gently push hand beneath skin and against meat to loosen.

Arrange a thyme sprig beneath skin on each drumstick. Arrange 2 sprigs each of thyme, rosemary, and sage beneath skin on breast. Gently press skin to secure.

Combine poultry seasoning, salt, and pepper. Sprinkle body cavity with half of seasoning mixture. Place 2 onion quarters, 4 celery pieces, and 1 sprig each of thyme, rosemary, and sage into body cavity. Repeat procedure for neck cavity. Tie ends of legs to tail with cord, or tuck them under flap of skin around tail. Lift wingtips up and over back, and tuck under turkey.

Place turkey, breast side up, on a rack coated with cooking spray; place rack in a shallow roasting pan. Coat turkey with cooking spray. Insert meat thermometer in meaty portion of thigh, making sure it does not touch bone. Cover loosely with aluminum foil, and bake at 325° for 2 hours. Uncover; bake an additional hour. Cut cord or band of skin holding drumstick ends to tail. Bake, uncovered, an additional 20 minutes or until meat thermometer registers 180°. Cover turkey loosely with foil; let stand 20 minutes. Place on a serving platter; garnish, if desired. Yield: 23 servings (about 144 calories per 3-ounce serving without skin).

"Food's neat; let's eat!" — Tommy's blessing

✦The Big Cut-Up à la Tommy Larson ✦

Any discussion of how to carve a turkey must begin with recalling how it all got started in the first place. In 1620, European dissidents fleeing religious persecution and shared bathrooms landed at Plymouth Rock, the site of America's first automobile dealership. They needed a name; after rejecting "Huddled Masses" and "Wretched Refuse," they settled on "Pilgrims" and proceeded to put buckles on their hats for no apparent reason.

They soon exhausted all the ship's rations and faced starvation. Then one resourceful Pilgrim yelled into the forest, "Hey! Any creatures out there willing to be roasted and eaten by 100 inebriated immigrants celebrating America's first automobile dealership?" Only the turkey, truly the stupidest of animals, volunteered. The rest is history.

You, as a dedicated automobile owner, doubtless want to keep this venerable tradition alive. Here's how to properly carve a turkey:

FIRST, place the turkey, breast side up, on a large platter. A few paper towels beneath the bird will keep it from accidentally scooting into the lap of a guest. Remove each leg by cutting the skin between it and the breast, pulling the leg away until it snaps at the joint and makes a fracturing sound reminiscent of the last time you tried to lift a refrigerator.

SECOND, cut through the connecting joint between the drumstick and thigh. If you get nervous, remember that surgeons do similar things to people who are merely anesthetized. You have a big advantage in that your patient is already dead.

THIRD, firmly secure the breast with a carving fork. Cut through the skin at the breastbone, and discard it. Place the knife parallel to the wing, and slice through the bottom of the breast to the ribs. At this point, your guests will be salivating, which is a good time to entertain bizarre suggestions about how the bird really died.

FOURTH, beginning at the outermost edge of the breast, slice down to the base cut. For fun, torture hungry guests by seeing how thin you can make each slice. Save the translucent slice for your unemployed brother-in-law, who's moved in with you until he starts up his mail-order nuclear waste business.

FINALLY, decide what to do with inevitable leftovers. Considering the special meaning of this day, you might donate them to your local automobile dealership. But be sure to cut everything into bite-size portions first, or you may be charged $27 an hour for labor.

Glorious Nutri-Bird, page 34

Dilly of Some Green Beans, page 40

Good Grief, Let's Eat
≻everything else≺

Marshmallow garnishes won't kill you if you only eat them once every 365 days. Just smile and say "delicious!" It's a small price for family harmony.

Dilly of Some Green Beans

2   pounds fresh green beans
2   teaspoons salt
²⁄₃   cup sliced green onions
¼   cup vegetable oil
1   tablespoon chopped fresh dillweed or 1 teaspoon dried
        dillweed
2   tablespoons red wine vinegar
1   teaspoon dry mustard
¼   teaspoon freshly ground pepper
Garnishes: pimiento strips and fresh dill sprigs

Wash beans; trim ends, and remove strings. Cut beans into
1½-inch pieces, if desired; set aside.

Add water to depth of 1 inch in a Dutch oven; bring to
a boil over high heat. Add beans and salt. Cover, reduce heat,
and simmer 10 to 12 minutes or until beans are crisp-tender.

Drain beans, and return to pan. Add green onions, and
keep warm.

Combine oil and next 4 ingredients; whisk vigorously.
Pour over bean mixture, and toss gently. Garnish, if desired.
Yield: 8 servings.

ɔccoli Casserole

ozen chopped broccoli, thawed
n of mushroom soup, undiluted
d sharp Cheddar cheese

en

nbs
d pimiento

by pressing it between paper
and next 5 ingredients. Spoon
ing dish. Top with cracker crumbs.
inutes. Garnish, if
gs.

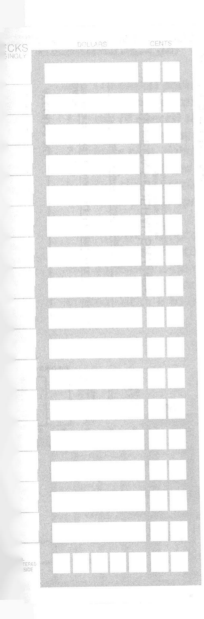

weet potatoes
e white meat

Orange-Kissed
Sweet Potatoes

8   medium-size sweet potatoes (about 4 pounds)
2   tablespoons grated orange rind
1   cup orange juice
⅓   cup sugar
⅓   cup firmly packed brown sugar
3   tablespoons butter or margarine, melted
1   tablespoon cornstarch
¼   teaspoon salt

Place washed sweet potatoes in a large Dutch oven; add
water to cover. Bring to a boil; cover, reduce heat to medium,
and simmer 25 to 30 minutes or until tender. Let cool to
touch; peel potatoes, and cut into ½-inch-thick slices.
Arrange potato slices in a lightly greased 13- x 9- x 2-inch
baking dish.
    Combine orange rind and remaining ingredients in a
small saucepan. Bring to a boil; boil 1 minute. Pour mixture
over sweet potato slices. Bake, uncovered, at 350° for 25 minutes or until thoroughly heated. Yield: 8 to 10 servings.

Note: Adele likes this recipe because she can prepare it ahead.
If you want to also, prepare it as directed, but do not bake.
Cover and refrigerate up to 8 hours. Remove from refrigerator;
let stand, covered, 20 minutes. Uncover and bake as directed.

Garlic Mashed Potatoes

3   pounds potatoes (about 4 large), *peeled*
2   (3-ounce) packages cream cheese
²/₃   cup sour cream
¼   cup milk
2   tablespoons butter or margarine
¾   teaspoon salt
3   cloves garlic, minced
1   tablespoon butter or margarine
½   teaspoon paprika

Cook potatoes in boiling salt[ed water 20] minutes or until tender; drain and mash [with a potato mash]er. Combine potato, cream cheese, and [other ingredients i]n a large mixing bowl; beat at medium s[peed with an electric] mixer until smooth.

Spoon mixture into a li[ghtly greased 13]- x 9- x 2-inch baking dish. Brush top of m[ixture with melt]ed butter; sprinkle with paprika. Bake at 350°, [uncovered, 25] minutes or until heated. Yield: 6 to 8 servings.

Note: Here's another dish Adele jumps the gun on. She covers this dish, unbaked, and chills it up to 24 hours. She always lets it sit at room temperature 20 minutes before baking it.

Carrot-Ambrosia Salad

1   pound carrots, scraped and shredded
1   (8-ounce) carton sour cream
1   (20-ounce) can crushed pineapple, drained
¾   cup golden raisins
¾   cup flaked coconut
¾   cup miniature marshmallows
2   tablespoons honey

Combine all ingredients, tossing well. Cover and chill at least 2 hours. Yield: 6 to 8 servings.

Annual Lime Salad Mold

1   (6-ounce) package lime-flavored gelatin
1   cup boiling water
1   cup cold water
1   (3-ounce) package cream cheese, softened
1   cup whipping cream, whipped
1   cup miniature marshmallows
1   cup chopped pecans
1   (8-ounce) can crushed pineapple, drained
Lettuce leaves

Dissolve gelatin in boiling water; stir in cold water. Beat cream cheese at medium speed of an electric mixer. Gradually beat in gelatin. Chill until consistency of unbeaten egg white. Fold whipped cream and next 3 ingredients into mixture. Pour into a shallow, lightly oiled 6-cup mold; cover and chill. Unmold onto a lettuce-lined plate, if desired. Yield: 12 servings.

Not-Thanksgiving-Without-It Cranberry Salad

2   *(3-ounce) packages raspberry-flavored gelatin*
1   *cup boiling water*
1   *cup cold water*
2   *cups fresh cranberries*
1   *cup pecan or walnut pieces*
2   *large, thin-skinned oranges, seeded and quartered*
1   *carrot, scraped and cut into 6 pieces*
1   *(8-ounce) can crushed pineapple, drained*
¾   *cup sugar*
Lettuce leaves
Garnish: carrot curls

Combine gelatin and boiling water, stirring 2 minutes or until gelatin dissolves. Add cold water, and chill until the consistency of unbeaten egg white.

Position knife blade in food processor bowl; add cranberries and next 3 ingredients. Pulse until mixture is finely chopped. Combine cranberry mixture, pineapple, and sugar, stirring well. Fold cranberry mixture into gelatin mixture. Pour into a lightly oiled 6½-cup mold. Cover and chill until firm. Unmold onto a lettuce-lined plate, and garnish, if desired. Yield: 8 servings.

Oyster-Bread Dressing

1   (1-pound) loaf French bread
¼   pound chicken gizzards
3   cups water
1¼ cups finely chopped onion
½   cup finely chopped celery
½   cup finely chopped green pepper
1   bunch fresh parsley, finely chopped
2   cloves garlic, crushed
¼   cup butter or margarine, melted
½   pound lean ground beef
¼   pound ground pork
¼   pound chicken livers, finely chopped
1   teaspoon instant-blending flour
½   teaspoon salt
¼   teaspoon black pepper
¼   teaspoon ground red pepper
⅛   teaspoon hot sauce
3   (12-ounce) containers Standard oysters, undrained

Cut bread in half lengthwise, and place, cut side up, on a baking sheet; bake bread at 350° for 15 to 20 minutes or until lightly browned. Cool. Tear bread into 1-inch pieces. Place in a large bowl, and set aside.

Place gizzards and water in a saucepan; cover and cook over medium heat 45 minutes or until tender. Remove gizzards, reserving 1½ cups broth. Finely chop gizzards; set aside.

Cook onion and next 4 ingredients in butter in a large skillet over medium heat, stirring constantly, until tender. Add gizzards, ground beef, pork, and liver; cook over medium-high heat until meat is no longer pink, stirring to crumble meat.

Add reserved 1½ cups broth; reduce heat to low, and simmer 30 minutes or until broth has been reduced to about ½ cup. Stir in flour and next 4 ingredients; simmer 10 minutes.

Spoon mixture over bread. Add oysters and liquid to bread mixture. Stir until blended. Spoon mixture into a well-greased, 13- x 9- x 2-inch baking dish. Bake, uncovered, at 350° for 30 to 40 minutes. Let stand 5 minutes. Yield: 8 servings.

Cornbread Dressing

2   *(6-ounce) packages cornbread mix*
1   *(5.5-ounce) can refrigerated buttermilk biscuits*
2¼ *cups chopped onion*
1½ *cups chopped celery*
¼   *cup butter or margarine, melted*
5½ *cups chicken broth*
5   *large eggs, lightly beaten*
1½ *teaspoons rubbed sage*
1½ *teaspoons pepper*
¾   *teaspoon salt*

Prepare cornbread mix and biscuits according to package directions; let cool. Crumble cornbread and biscuits in a large bowl. Set aside.

Cook onion and celery in butter in a skillet over medium-high heat, stirring constantly, until tender. Add onion mixture, broth, and remaining ingredients to cornbread mixture; stir well. Spoon mixture into a greased 13- x 9- x 2-inch baking dish; bake, uncovered, at 350° for 55 minutes or until golden. Yield: 8 to 10 servings.

Cranberry-Orange Relish

4   cups fresh cranberries
2   cups sugar
½   cup water
½   cup orange juice
⅓   cup slivered almonds, toasted

Combine first 4 ingredients; bring to a boil. Reduce heat, and simmer 10 minutes, stirring occasionally. Cover and chill. Stir in almonds just before serving. Yield: 3½ cups.

Tabbouleh Skillet

1   tablespoon olive oil
1   cup bulgur (cracked wheat), uncooked
½   cup chopped green pepper
½   cup sliced green onions
1   clove garlic, minced
2   cups water
2   teaspoons lemon juice
¼   teaspoon salt
¼   teaspoon dried marjoram
⅛   teaspoon pepper
1   cup chopped yellow squash
1   cup chopped tomato

Heat oil in a skillet. Add bulgur and next 3 ingredients; cook, stirring constantly, 3 minutes. Add next 5 ingredients; cover and cook 15 minutes. Stir in squash and tomato. Cover; cook 5 minutes. Yield: 10 servings (71 calories per ½-cup serving).

Pasta e Fagioli

1¼ cups dried Great Northern beans
2 quarts water
Olive oil-flavored vegetable cooking spray
1 teaspoon olive oil
½ cup finely chopped red onion
¼ cup finely chopped celery
1 tablespoon minced garlic
2 teaspoons chopped fresh rosemary
2 teaspoons chopped fresh sage
1 cup peeled, seeded, and finely chopped tomato
¼ teaspoon salt
1 teaspoon pepper
8 ounces ditalini pasta, uncooked
3 cups coarsely chopped fresh spinach

Sort and wash beans; place in a Dutch oven. Cover with water to a depth of 2 inches above beans; cover and let soak 8 hours. Drain and rinse beans.

Combine beans and 2 quarts water in pan. Bring to a boil; cover, reduce heat, and simmer 1 hour. Transfer 2 cups beans, without liquid, to container of an electric blender or food processor; cover and process until smooth. Return to pan.

Coat a large nonstick skillet with cooking spray; add oil. Place over medium heat until hot; add onion and next 4 ingredients, and cook, stirring constantly, 5 minutes. Add onion mixture, tomato, salt, and pepper to bean mixture. Cook over medium-low heat 15 minutes. Add pasta, and cook 20 additional minutes, stirring frequently. Add spinach, and cook 2 minutes or until spinach wilts. Yield: 8 servings (261 calories per 1-cup serving).

New England Bread Dressing

12   cups (½-inch) cubes white bread
2   tablespoons margarine
1½   cups chopped celery
1   cup chopped onion
2   tablespoons water
1   tablespoon sugar
2½   teaspoons poultry seasoning
¾   teaspoon dried basil
¼   teaspoon salt
¼   teaspoon ground nutmeg
¼   teaspoon pepper
1   cup low-sodium chicken broth
1   large egg, lightly beaten
Vegetable cooking spray

Place bread cubes on a 15- x 10- x 1-inch jellyroll pan; bake at 325° for 20 minutes or until toasted. Set aside.

Melt margarine in a large skillet over medium heat. Add celery, onion, and water; cover, reduce heat, and cook 15 minutes or until tender. Remove from heat. Stir in sugar and next 5 ingredients.

Combine bread cubes, celery mixture, broth, and egg in a bowl; stir well. Spoon mixture into a 2-quart baking dish coated with cooking spray. Bake, uncovered, at 325° for 35 minutes. Yield: 8 servings (221 calories per 1-cup serving).

Creamy Sage-Giblet Gravy

1   teaspoon vegetable oil
2¹/₂   ounces turkey liver
1   cup degreased turkey drippings
3   tablespoons all-purpose flour
1²/₃   cups 2% low-fat milk
¹/₂   cup evaporated skim milk
1¹/₂   teaspoons margarine
1   teaspoon rubbed sage
1   small clove garlic, minced
2   tablespoons chopped fresh parsley
1   teaspoon spicy brown mustard
¹/₂   teaspoon salt

Heat oil in a small nonstick skillet over medium heat. Add liver; cook, stirring constantly, 5 minutes or until done. Remove from skillet; set aside. Add drippings to skillet; bring to a boil, stirring with a wooden spoon to loosen browned bits. Remove from heat; set aside. Chop liver; set aside.

Place flour in a bowl. Gradually add milks, blending with a wire whisk; set aside. Melt margarine in a large saucepan over medium heat. Add sage and garlic; cook, stirring constantly, 1 minute. Add milk mixture, stirring constantly. Stir in drippings and liver; bring to a boil, stirring constantly. Reduce heat, and simmer, uncovered, 2 minutes or until thickened. Remove from heat; stir in parsley, mustard, and salt. Yield: 3¹/₂ cups (72 calories per ¹/₃-cup serving).

Golden Carrots

4	cups thinly sliced carrots
1	cup unsweetened pineapple juice
1	cup water
2	teaspoons grated lemon rind
½	cup golden raisins
2	teaspoons reduced-calorie margarine
1	teaspoon vanilla extract
½	teaspoon ground mace

Combine first 4 ingredients in a saucepan; bring to a boil. Cover, reduce heat, and simmer 10 to 12 minutes or just until tender. Remove from heat; drain carrots, reserving ¼ cup liquid. Stir reserved liquid and remaining ingredients into carrots. Yield: 8 servings (80 calories per serving).

"Don't comment on things you don't understand."

Sweet Corn Niblets

6   cups fresh corn cut from cob (about 12 ears)
1½ cups water
½   cup chopped green onions
¼   cup chopped green pepper
2   tablespoons chopped fresh basil
2   tablespoons white wine vinegar
½   teaspoon sugar
¼   teaspoon salt
¼   teaspoon ground white pepper
¼   teaspoon hot sauce
Garnish: fresh basil sprigs

Combine corn, water, green onions, and green pepper in a medium saucepan. Bring to a boil; reduce heat, and simmer, uncovered, 20 minutes. Add chopped basil and next 5 ingredients; cook 10 minutes or until corn is tender. Transfer to a serving bowl; garnish, if desired. Serve with a slotted spoon. Yield: 10 servings (84 calories per ½-cup serving).

Tipsy Taters au Gratin

2   large onions (about 2 pounds)
Vegetable cooking spray
2   teaspoons vegetable oil
1⅓ cups sweet Marsala wine
1   teaspoon dried thyme
2½ pounds medium-size round red potatoes, peeled and cut
       into ⅛-inch slices
2   tablespoons all-purpose flour
¾   teaspoon salt
½   cup skim milk
2   tablespoons grated Parmesan cheese

Cut each onion in half lengthwise, and cut each half crosswise into ⅛-inch-thick slices. Coat a large saucepan with cooking spray; add oil, and place over medium heat until hot. Add onion, and cook, stirring constantly, 10 minutes. Add wine; cook 20 minutes or until liquid is nearly absorbed, stirring frequently. Remove from heat; stir in thyme. Set aside.

Cook potato slices in boiling water 8 minutes or until crisp-tender; drain. Pour cold water over potato slices; drain.

Arrange one-third of potato slices in a 13- x 9- x 2-inch baking dish coated with cooking spray, and spoon half of onion mixture over potato slices. Repeat procedure with remaining potato slices and onion mixture, ending with potato slices.

Place flour and salt in a bowl. Gradually add milk, blending with a wire whisk until smooth. Pour mixture evenly over potato slices; sprinkle with cheese. Cover with aluminum foil, and cut 3 (1-inch) slits in foil. Bake at 350° for 45 minutes. Uncover and bake 15 additional minutes. Yield: 7 servings (156 calories per 1-cup serving).

Tipsy Taters au Gratin, facing page

Anytime Refrigerator Rolls, page 58, Cheesy Herb Loaves, page 59

Positive Roll Models
❖breads❖

It's a good idea to take a roll when it's passed to you, even though you don't intend to eat it. If a food fight breaks out, this is the food to wing at your loved ones. Remember, no nut breads. You could put somebody's eye out.

Anytime Refrigerator Rolls

½   cup sugar
1   cup buttermilk
¾   cup shortening
1   teaspoon salt
1   cup cooked, mashed potatoes
2   packages active dry yeast
¼   cup warm water (105° to 115°)
2   large eggs
4¾ to 5¼ cups all-purpose flour, divided
Butter or margarine, melted

Combine first 4 ingredients in a saucepan; heat until shortening melts. Remove from heat; stir in potatoes. Cool to 105° to 115°. Dissolve yeast in warm water in a large mixing bowl; let stand 5 minutes. Add potato mixture, eggs, and 2 cups flour, beating at medium speed of an electric mixer until smooth. Gradually stir in enough remaining flour to make a soft dough.

Turn dough out onto a floured surface; knead until smooth and elastic (8 minutes). Place in a greased bowl, turning to grease top. Cover and chill 3 hours or until doubled. (May be kept in refrigerator up to 1 week.)

Punch dough down; divide into thirds. Roll 1 third into a 10-inch circle on a floured surface; brush with butter. Cut into 12 wedges; roll up wedges from wide end. Place on greased baking sheet, point side down. Repeat with remaining dough, or cover and chill up to 1 week. Cover and let rise in a warm place (85°), free from drafts, 50 minutes or until doubled. Bake at 425° for 6 minutes or until golden. Yield: 3 dozen.

Cheesy Herb Loaves

1 cup milk
3 tablespoons sugar
2 tablespoons shortening
1½ teaspoons salt
2 packages active dry yeast
1 cup warm water (105° to 115°)
1 large egg, lightly beaten
5¼ to 5¾ cups all-purpose flour, divided
2 cups (8 ounces) shredded sharp Cheddar cheese
¾ teaspoon dried basil
½ teaspoon rubbed sage

Combine first 4 ingredients in a saucepan; heat until shortening melts. Cool to 105° to 115°. Dissolve yeast in warm water in a large bowl; let stand 5 minutes. Add milk mixture, egg, and 2 cups flour, stirring until smooth. Stir in cheese and herbs; gradually stir in enough remaining flour to make a soft dough. Cover and let stand 10 minutes.

Turn dough out onto a lightly floured surface; knead until smooth and elastic (8 to 10 minutes). Place in a greased bowl, turning to grease top. Cover and let rise in a warm place (85°), free from drafts, 45 minutes or until doubled in bulk.

Punch dough down; divide in half. Shape each portion into a loaf, and place in two greased 9- x 5- x 3-inch loafpans. Cover and let rise in a warm place, free from drafts, 30 minutes or until doubled in bulk. Bake at 375° for 30 minutes or until loaves sound hollow when tapped. Remove from pans immediately; let cool on wire racks. Yield: 2 loaves.

Candy Cane Bread

1½ cups chopped dried apricots
2   cups boiling water
1   (16-ounce) carton sour cream
⅓   cup sugar
¼   cup butter or margarine
1½ teaspoons salt
2   packages active dry yeast
½   cup warm water (105° to 115°)
2   large eggs
6   to 6½ cups all-purpose flour, divided
1½ cups chopped maraschino cherries
¼   cup butter or margarine, melted
1   cup sifted powdered sugar
1   tablespoon plus 1 to 2 teaspoons milk
Garnish: candied cherry halves

Combine apricots and boiling water; cover and let stand 1
hour. Drain well, and set apricots aside.

Combine sour cream, sugar, ¼ cup butter, and salt in a
heavy saucepan; stir over low heat until butter melts. Cool
to 105° to 115°. Dissolve yeast in warm water in a large
mixing bowl; let stand 5 minutes. Add sour cream mixture,
eggs, and 2 cups flour, beating at low speed of an electric
mixer until smooth. Stir in enough remaining flour to make
a soft dough.

Turn dough out onto a lightly floured surface; knead
until smooth and elastic (8 to 10 minutes). Place dough in
a greased bowl, turning to grease top. Cover and let rise in
a warm place (85°), free from drafts, 1 hour or until doubled
in bulk.

Punch dough down; divide into thirds. Roll each portion into a 15- x 6-inch rectangle on a lightly floured surface; transfer to greased baking sheets. Make 2-inch cuts into dough at ½-inch intervals on long sides of rectangle, leaving a 2-inch uncut strip down the center. Combine apricots and maraschino cherries; spread down center of dough rectangles. Fold and overlap strips diagonally over fruit filling in a braided fashion; gently stretch dough to measure 22 inches. Curve one end to resemble a cane.

Bake at 375° for 15 minutes or until golden. Brush each cane with melted butter; let cool. Combine powdered sugar and enough milk to make a glaze of desired consistency; stir until smooth, and drizzle over bread. Garnish, if desired. Yield: 3 loaves.

"I pick myself up ... I dust myself off ... and start all over again."

Chunky Chocolate Bread

½   cup water
¼   cup butter or margarine
¼   cup sugar
1   package active dry yeast
¼   cup warm water (105° to 115°)
3   to 3½ cups all-purpose flour, divided
3   tablespoons cocoa
¾   teaspoon salt
⅛   teaspoon ground cinnamon
2   large eggs
1   teaspoon vanilla extract
½   cup semisweet chocolate chunks
Glaze

Combine first 3 ingredients in a saucepan; heat until butter melts. Cool to 105° to 115°. Dissolve yeast in ¼ cup warm water in a large mixing bowl; let stand 5 minutes. Add butter mixture, 2 cups flour, cocoa, salt, cinnamon, eggs, and vanilla; beat at low speed of an electric mixer 30 seconds. Beat 3 additional minutes at medium speed. Gradually stir in enough remaining flour to make a soft dough.

Turn dough out onto a lightly floured surface; knead until smooth and elastic (8 to 10 minutes). Place in a greased bowl, turning to grease top. Cover and let rise in a warm place (85°), free from drafts, 1 hour or until doubled in bulk.

Punch dough down, and turn out onto a floured surface; roll into an 18- x 10-inch rectangle. Sprinkle dough with chocolate chunks, pressing chunks gently into dough. Roll up dough, jellyroll fashion, starting at one short end. Fold ends under, and place seam side down in a greased 9- x 5- x 3-inch loafpan. Cover and let rise in a warm place, free from drafts, 45 minutes or until doubled in bulk. Bake at 350° for 30 minutes or until loaf sounds hollow when tapped. Remove bread from pan immediately; let cool on a wire rack. Drizzle Glaze over loaf. Yield: 1 loaf.

Glaze

1   cup sifted powdered sugar
1½ tablespoons milk
½   teaspoon vanilla extract

Combine all ingredients, stirring well. Yield: about ⅓ cup.

"This has been ... what has this been? This has been a complete happy holiday nightmare."

Lemon Loveknots

1   cup milk
⅓   cup sugar
½   cup shortening
1   teaspoon salt
1   package active dry yeast
¼   cup warm water (105° to 115°)
2   large eggs
¼   cup milk
1   tablespoon grated lemon rind
5   to 5½ cups all-purpose flour, divided
1   cup sifted powdered sugar
1   to 2 tablespoons milk
1   teaspoon grated lemon rind

Combine first 4 ingredients in a saucepan; heat until shortening melts. Cool to 105° to 115°. Dissolve yeast in warm water in a large mixing bowl; let stand 5 minutes. Add milk mixture, eggs, ¼ cup milk, 1 tablespoon lemon rind, and 3 cups flour, beating at medium speed of an electric mixer until smooth. Gradually stir in enough remaining flour to make a soft dough. Cover and let stand 10 minutes.

Turn dough out onto a lightly floured surface; knead until smooth and elastic (about 5 minutes). Place in a greased bowl, turning to grease top. Cover and let rise in a warm place (85°), free from drafts, 1 to 1½ hours or until doubled in bulk.

Punch dough down; cover and let stand 15 minutes. Roll dough into an 18- x 10-inch rectangle. Cut dough into 24 (10- x ¾-inch) strips. Roll each strip back and forth lightly in hands to make into rope; tie loosely into a knot. Place on greased baking sheets. Cover and let rise in a warm place, free from drafts, 35 minutes or until doubled in bulk. Bake at 400° for 10 to 12 minutes or until golden.

Combine powdered sugar, 1 tablespoon milk, and 1 teaspoon lemon rind, stirring well. Add more milk, if needed, to make glaze desired consistency. Brush glaze on loveknots. Yield: 2 dozen.

Merry Muffins

2   cups all-purpose flour
2   teaspoons baking powder
½   teaspoon salt
½   cup sugar
⅔   cup chopped pecans
1   large egg, lightly beaten
¾   cup milk
⅓   cup vegetable oil
¼   cup chocolate-flavored drink mix
¼   cup chopped maraschino cherries
Powdered sugar (optional)

Combine first 5 ingredients in a large bowl, stirring well; make a well in center of flour mixture. Combine egg, milk, and vegetable oil; add to dry ingredients, stirring just until moistened.

Divide batter in half; stir chocolate drink mix into 1 portion and cherries into remaining portion. Spoon about 1 tablespoon chocolate batter into one side of each greased muffin cup and about 1 tablespoon cherry batter into other side. Bake at 400° for 15 minutes or until golden. Remove from pans immediately. Sprinkle with powdered sugar, if desired. Yield: 14 muffins.

Cinnamon-Raisin Pastries

2   (8-ounce) packages cream cheese, softened
1   cup butter, softened
1   cup margarine, softened
6   cups all-purpose flour
Powdered sugar
Raisin Filling

Combine cream cheese, butter, and margarine in a large
mixing bowl; beat at medium speed of an electric mixer
until smooth. Add flour; mix well. Divide dough into 4 equal
portions. Roll 1 portion of dough into a 12- x 9-inch rectangle
on a surface lightly sprinkled with powdered sugar; cut into
12 (3-inch) squares. Spoon about 2 teaspoons Raisin Filling
onto each square, leaving a ½-inch margin. Roll squares
jellyroll fashion; place seam side down on ungreased baking
sheets.

Bake at 375° for 20 minutes or until lightly browned.
Cool on wire racks. Repeat with remaining dough and filling.
Yield: 4 dozen.

Raisin Filling

¾   cup raisins
1¼ cups hot water
1½ cups ground pecans
¾   cup sugar
1½ teaspoons ground cinnamon

Combine raisins and water, and let stand 15 minutes.
Drain raisins.

Combine raisins, pecans, sugar, and cinnamon; stir well. Yield: 2⅔ cups.

Note: Sometimes Adele freezes these pastries in an airtight container before baking. She then thaws them at room temperature and bakes as directed in recipe.

Unbelievable Biscuit Muffins

1½ cups all-purpose flour
2   teaspoons baking powder
½   teaspoon baking soda
¼   teaspoon salt
1   cup low-fat sour cream
1   large egg, lightly beaten
1   tablespoon vegetable oil
Vegetable cooking spray

Combine first 4 ingredients in a medium bowl; make a well in center of mixture. Combine sour cream, egg, and oil; add to dry ingredients, stirring just until moistened. Spoon batter into muffin pans coated with cooking spray, filling two-thirds full. Bake at 400° for 15 minutes or until lightly browned. Remove from pans immediately. Yield: 1 dozen (98 calories per muffin).

Whole Grain-Pumpkin Muffins

¾ cup shreds of wheat bran cereal
¾ cup nonfat buttermilk
½ cup cooked, mashed pumpkin
¼ cup vegetable oil
1 large egg, lightly beaten
1 teaspoon grated orange rind
¾ cup all-purpose flour
¾ cup whole wheat flour
½ teaspoon baking powder
½ teaspoon baking soda
⅛ teaspoon salt
1 teaspoon ground cinnamon
⅓ cup sugar
Vegetable cooking spray
1 tablespoon sugar
¼ teaspoon ground cinnamon

Combine cereal and buttermilk in a bowl; let stand 5 minutes. Add pumpkin, oil, egg, and orange rind; stir well. Combine all-purpose flour and next 6 ingredients in a large bowl; make a well in center of mixture. Add buttermilk mixture, stirring just until dry ingredients are moistened (batter will be thick).

Spoon batter into muffin pans coated with cooking spray, filling two-thirds full. Combine 1 tablespoon sugar and ¼ teaspoon cinnamon; sprinkle evenly over muffins. Bake at 400° for 15 to 20 minutes or until golden. Yield: 1 dozen (142 calories per muffin).

Light Cranberry-Orange Bread

2	cups whole wheat flour
½	cup sugar
¼	cup instant nonfat dry milk powder
1	teaspoon baking powder
1	teaspoon baking soda
¼	teaspoon salt
¼	cup margarine, melted
2	large eggs, lightly beaten
1	cup unsweetened orange juice
¼	cup chopped walnuts
1½	cups fresh cranberries, coarsely chopped

Vegetable cooking spray

Combine first 6 ingredients in a large bowl; make a well in center of mixture. Whisk together margarine, eggs, and orange juice; add to dry ingredients, stirring just until moistened. Stir in walnuts and cranberries.

Spoon batter into a 9- x 5- x 3-inch loafpan coated with cooking spray. Bake at 350° for 1 hour or until a wooden pick inserted in center comes out clean. Cool in pan on a wire rack 10 minutes; remove bread from pan, and let cool on a wire rack. Yield: 18 servings (125 calories per ½-inch slice).

Stollen à la Larson

¼ cup candied orange peel
¼ cup coarsely chopped red candied cherries
¼ cup currants
¼ cup golden raisins
2 tablespoons brandy
1 tablespoon vanilla extract
½ cup 1% low-fat milk
¼ cup plus 1 tablespoon sugar, divided
2 tablespoons margarine
1 package active dry yeast
2 tablespoons warm water (105° to 115°)
2½ to 3 cups all-purpose flour, divided
1 teaspoon grated lemon rind
½ teaspoon ground nutmeg
1 large egg
½ cup slivered almonds, toasted
Vegetable cooking spray
½ cup sifted powdered sugar
2 teaspoons 1% low-fat milk

Combine orange peel, cherries, currants, raisins, brandy, and vanilla extract in a small bowl; let stand 2 hours, stirring occasionally. Drain and set aside.

Heat ½ cup milk over medium-high heat in a heavy saucepan to 180° or until tiny bubbles form around the edge. (Do not boil.) Remove from heat; add ¼ cup sugar and margarine, stirring until margarine melts. Let cool.

Dissolve yeast and 1 teaspoon sugar in 2 tablespoons warm water in a large mixing bowl; let stand 5 minutes. Add milk mixture, 1 cup flour, and next 3 ingredients. Beat at low speed of an electric mixer 2 minutes or until smooth. Stir in 1 cup flour, ½ cup at a time, to form a soft dough.

Turn dough out onto a lightly floured surface. Knead until smooth and elastic (about 8 minutes); add enough flour, 1 tablespoon at a time, to prevent dough from sticking to hands. Combine fruit mixture, almonds, and 1 tablespoon flour; stir well. Add fruit mixture to dough in 2 batches, kneading until all fruit is combined; add enough remaining flour, 1 tablespoon at a time, to prevent dough from sticking to hands. Place dough in a large bowl coated with cooking spray, turning to coat top of dough. Cover and let rise in a warm place (85°), free from drafts, 1 hour or until doubled in bulk.

Punch dough down; let stand 5 minutes. Turn dough out onto a lightly floured surface; roll into a 12- x 8-inch rectangle. Sprinkle 1½ teaspoons sugar over entire surface. Fold dough in half lengthwise, leaving a ½-inch margin; pinch seam to seal. Sprinkle with remaining ½ teaspoon sugar. Place dough, seam side up, on a baking sheet coated with cooking spray.

Cover and let rise in a warm place (85°), free from drafts, 30 minutes or until doubled in bulk. Bake at 350° for 20 minutes. Reduce heat to 300°; continue baking 15 minutes or until loaf sounds hollow when tapped. Let cool on a wire rack.

Combine powdered sugar and 2 teaspoons milk; stir well. Drizzle over loaf. Yield: 26 servings (about 110 calories per ½-inch slice).

Italian Dinner Rolls

2   packages active dry yeast
2   tablespoons sugar
2   cups warm water (105° to 115°)
4½   cups bread flour
½   cup grated Parmesan cheese
1   teaspoon dried Italian seasoning
½   teaspoon salt
3   tablespoons bread flour, divided
1   teaspoon cornmeal

Dissolve yeast and sugar in warm water in a large mixing bowl; let stand 5 minutes. Combine 4½ cups flour, cheese, Italian seasoning, and salt. Add 3 cups flour mixture to yeast mixture, beating at medium speed of an electric mixer until blended. Gradually stir in enough of remaining flour mixture to make a soft dough. Cover and let rest 15 minutes.

Sprinkle 2 tablespoons flour evenly over work surface. Turn dough out onto floured surface, and knead until smooth and elastic (8 to 10 minutes), using remaining 1 tablespoon flour for kneading, if necessary.

Divide dough into 20 equal portions; shape each portion into a ball. Place on an ungreased baking sheet sprinkled with 1 teaspoon cornmeal. Gently cut a ¼-inch-deep slit across top of each ball with a razor blade or sharp knife.

Cover and let rise in a warm place (85°), free from drafts, 35 minutes or until doubled in bulk. Place a 13- x 9- x 2-inch pan of boiling water on lower rack of oven. Place baking sheet on rack in middle of oven. Bake at 400° for 15 minutes or until golden. Remove from baking sheet; let cool on wire racks. Yield: 20 rolls (115 calories per roll).

Stollen à la Larson, page 70

Harvest Pumpkin Pie, page 76

A Tradition of Mind-Numbing Excess
❧desserts❧

"Please! No way, José. I couldn't possibly. Don't be ridiculous. I know you slaved over a hot stove and it's my favorite—maybe in a couple of hours . . . jeeze, it smells great, though. Just give me a tiny bit and no ice cream."

Harvest Pumpkin Pie

Pastry for double-crust pie
3   *cups cooked, mashed pumpkin*
1   *(12-ounce) can evaporated milk*
2   *large eggs, lightly beaten*
1   *cup sugar*
¼   *cup all-purpose flour*
1   *teaspoon vanilla extract*
½   *teaspoon salt*
½   *teaspoon ground allspice*
½   *teaspoon ground cinnamon*
½   *teaspoon ground ginger*
¼   *teaspoon ground cloves*
¼   *teaspoon ground nutmeg*
1   *cup whipping cream*
2   *tablespoons honey*
2   *tablespoons finely chopped pecans, toasted*

Roll half of pastry to ⅛-inch thickness on a lightly floured surface. Place in a 10-inch pieplate. Roll remaining pastry to ⅛-inch thickness; cut leaf shapes in pastry, making vein markings with the back of a knife. Arrange leaves around the edge of pieplate, reserving 6 small leaves for garnish. Set aside.

Combine pumpkin and next 11 ingredients in a large bowl; stir well with a wire whisk. Pour pumpkin mixture into prepared pastry. Bake at 425° for 15 minutes. Reduce heat to 350°, and bake 35 to 45 additional minutes or until a knife inserted near center comes out clean. Shield pastry leaves with strips of aluminum foil to prevent excess browning, if necessary. Remove pie from oven, and let cool completely on a wire rack.

Place reserved pastry leaves on an ungreased baking sheet. Bake at 450° for 6 to 8 minutes or until lightly browned. Remove to a wire rack, and let cool.

Beat whipping cream at high speed of an electric mixer until stiff peaks form; fold in honey. Garnish pie with dollops of sweetened whipped cream. Sprinkle pecans over whipped cream. Garnish with small pastry leaves. Yield: one 10-inch pie.

Key Lime Pie

⅓   cup Key lime juice
1   (14-ounce) can sweetened condensed milk
⅓   cup sifted powdered sugar
1½   teaspoons grated lime rind
1   (9-inch) graham cracker crust
3   egg whites
¼   teaspoon cream of tartar
¼   cup plus 2 tablespoons sugar
Garnish: candy-coated chocolate pieces

Stir lime juice gradually into sweetened condensed milk; stir in powdered sugar and lime rind. Spoon filling into graham cracker crust; set aside.

Beat egg whites and cream of tartar at high speed of an electric mixer 1 minute. Add sugar, 1 tablespoon at a time, beating until stiff peaks form and sugar dissolves (2 to 4 minutes). Spread meringue over filling, sealing to edge of pastry. Bake at 325° for 25 to 30 minutes or until golden. Cool on a wire rack; chill. Garnish, if desired. Yield: one 9-inch pie.

Tipsy Pecan Pie

½	cup butter or margarine, melted
1	cup sugar
1	cup light corn syrup
3	tablespoons bourbon
4	large eggs, lightly beaten
1	teaspoon vanilla extract
¼	teaspoon salt
1	unbaked 9-inch pastry shell
1	to 1¼ cups pecan halves

Combine butter, sugar, and corn syrup in a medium saucepan; cook over low heat, stirring constantly, until sugar dissolves. Let cool slightly. Add bourbon, eggs, vanilla, and salt to mixture; mix well.

Pour filling into unbaked pastry shell, and top with pecan halves. Bake at 325° for 50 to 55 minutes. Serve warm or cold. Yield: one 9-inch pie.

"Can't you empty the dishwasher first?"

Cherry-Berry Pie

1	*(16-ounce) can pitted red cherries, undrained*
1	*(10-ounce) package frozen red raspberries, thawed*
1	*cup sugar*
¼	*cup cornstarch*
¼	*cup butter or margarine*
¼	*teaspoon almond extract*
¼	*teaspoon red liquid food coloring*
1	*(15-ounce) package refrigerated piecrusts*
1	*teaspoon all-purpose flour*

Garnishes: fresh raspberries and powdered sugar

Drain cherries and raspberries, reserving 1 cup combined juices; set fruit aside. Combine sugar and cornstarch in a medium saucepan; gradually stir in 1 cup reserved juice. Cook over medium heat, stirring constantly, until mixture begins to boil. Cook 1 minute, stirring constantly. Remove from heat; stir in butter, almond extract, and food coloring. Gently fold in reserved fruit; cool slightly.

Unfold 1 piecrust, and press out fold lines; sprinkle with flour, spreading over surface. Place, floured side down, in a 9-inch pieplate; fold edges under, and flute. Spoon in filling. Roll remaining piecrust to press out fold lines. Cut 5 leaves with a 3¼-inch leaf-shaped cutter, and mark veins using a pastry wheel or knife; set aside. Cut remaining pastry into ½-inch strips, and arrange in a lattice design over filling. Top with pastry leaves. Bake at 375° for 45 minutes. Cool on a wire rack. Garnish, if desired. Yield: one 9-inch pie.

Lemon-Raspberry Cake

1   cup shortening
2   cups sugar
4   large eggs
3   cups sifted cake flour
2½   teaspoons baking powder
½   teaspoon salt
1   cup milk
1   teaspoon almond extract
1   teaspoon vanilla extract
1   (10-ounce) jar seedless raspberry preserves
Lemon Buttercream Frosting
Garnish: lemon slice wedges

Grease 3 (9-inch) round cakepans; line with wax paper. Grease and flour wax paper. Set pans aside.

Beat shortening in a large mixing bowl at medium speed of an electric mixer until creamy; gradually add sugar, beating well. Add eggs, one at a time, beating after each addition. Combine flour, baking powder, and salt; add flour mixture to shortening mixture alternately with milk, beginning and ending with flour mixture. Mix at low speed after each addition. Stir in flavorings.

Pour batter into prepared pans. Bake at 375° for 18 to 20 minutes or until a wooden pick inserted in center comes out clean. Cool in pans on wire racks 10 minutes; remove from pans, and let cool completely on wire racks.

Slice cake layers in half horizontally to make 6 layers. Place 1 layer, cut side up, on a cake plate, and spread with 3 tablespoons preserves. Repeat procedure with remaining 5 layers and preserves, omitting preserves on top of last layer.

Reserve 1 cup Lemon Buttercream Frosting; spread remaining frosting on top and sides of cake. Using a star tip, pipe reserved frosting on top of cake. Garnish, if desired. Store in an airtight container in refrigerator. Yield: one 6-layer cake.

Lemon Buttercream Frosting

1¼ cups butter or margarine, softened
2 teaspoons grated lemon rind
3 tablespoons lemon juice
3 cups sifted powdered sugar

Beat first 3 ingredients in a small mixing bowl at medium speed of an electric mixer until creamy. Gradually add powdered sugar, beating until frosting is spreading consistency. Yield: 2¾ cups.

"I'm taking a huge chance here, because that's what life's about . . ."

White Ambrosia Cake

1   cup butter or margarine, softened
2   cups sugar
4   large eggs
3   cups sifted cake flour
2½ teaspoons baking powder
½   teaspoon salt
1   cup milk
1   teaspoon butter flavoring
1   teaspoon vanilla extract
Orange Filling
Divinity Frosting
½   cup flaked coconut

Beat butter in a large mixing bowl at medium speed of an electric mixer until creamy; gradually add sugar, beating well. Add eggs, one at a time, beating after each addition. Combine flour, baking powder, and salt; add to butter mixture alternately with milk, beginning and ending with flour mixture. Mix at low speed after each addition until blended. Stir in flavorings.

Pour batter into 3 greased and floured 9-inch round cakepans. Bake at 350° for 20 to 25 minutes or until a wooden pick inserted in center comes out clean. Cool in pans on wire racks 10 minutes; remove from pans, and let cool completely on wire racks.

Spread Orange Filling between layers. Spread top and sides of cake with Divinity Frosting, and sprinkle coconut evenly on top. Yield: one 3-layer cake.

Orange Filling

1   cup sugar
3   tablespoons cornstarch
¾   cup orange juice
¼   cup lemon juice
⅓   cup water
3   egg yolks
1   tablespoon grated orange rind

Combine sugar and cornstarch in a saucepan. Combine juices and water; gradually add to sugar mixture. Cook, stirring constantly, until mixture comes to a boil; boil 1 minute.

Beat egg yolks until thick and pale. Gradually stir about one-fourth of hot mixture into yolks; add to remaining hot mixture, stirring constantly. Cook, stirring constantly, 1 minute. Stir in orange rind. Cool. Yield: about 2 cups.

Divinity Frosting

1½   cups sugar
½   teaspoon cream of tartar
½   cup water
3   egg whites
½   teaspoon vanilla extract

Combine first 3 ingredients in a heavy saucepan. Cook over medium heat, stirring constantly, until mixture is clear. Cook, without stirring, until candy thermometer registers 240°.

Beat egg whites at high speed of an electric mixer until soft peaks form. With mixer running, add syrup mixture in a heavy stream. Add vanilla; beat until stiff peaks form and frosting is spreading consistency. Yield: enough for one 3-layer cake.

Hazel Radant's

⁕ Criminally Easy Cobbler ⁕

Preheat oven to 350°

• Spray 7" square baking pan with Pam. (The pan can actually be any shape, including parallelogram, like the one we used to prop the garage door open with.)

• Open a can of fruit pie filling, and dump it into the lubricated pan so it makes the sound "poit."

• Spread the filling flat with the back side of a large spoon, and then lick it clean. Spread a second time if necessary.

• Evenly sprinkle your choice of yellow, white, lemon or white cake mix on top of the pie filling in a ½" layer. Clumps are good. Should resemble surface of moon.

• Crumbled pecans or walnuts optional, but recommended for added calories.

• Place pads of butter about an index finger's length apart on top of the cake mix moon surface.

• Bake at 350° for oh, I don't know, about 20 minutes or until golden brown and convincingly cobblerish.

• Serve piping hot with a blob of ice cream. (Refuse to divulge recipe.)

• Serves 6 regular people or 3 or 4 Radants.

⁕ Hazel Radant is the criminally easy-cooking mother of Christine Radant, author of easy-reading words throughout this book and author of the original short story, *Home for the Holidays*. Many thanks to both.

Cranberry Squares

½   cup butter or margarine, softened
1   (8-ounce) can almond paste
1   cup sugar
2   large eggs
3¼ cups all-purpose flour
¼   teaspoon salt
2   (9-ounce) jars raspberry-cranberry fruit spread

Beat butter and almond paste at medium speed of an electric mixer until smooth; add sugar and eggs, beating well. Combine flour and salt; gradually add to almond mixture, beating well. Set aside 1½ cups.

Spread remaining almond mixture in a lightly greased 15- x 10- x 1-inch jellyroll pan. Spread evenly with raspberry-cranberry spread. Chill.

Roll reserved almond mixture between 2 sheets of wax paper to ⅛-inch thickness. Place on a baking sheet; freeze 15 minutes. Remove top piece of wax paper; cut into desired shapes with a 1½-inch canapé cutter. Place cutouts over cranberry mixture. Bake at 350° on lowest oven rack for 40 minutes or until lightly browned. Cool and cut into squares. Store in an airtight container up to 3 days. Yield: 4½ dozen.

Note: For fruit spread, Adele uses Knott's Berry Farm Light Raspberry and Cranberry Fruit Spread.

Braided Candy Canes

¾ cup butter or margarine, softened
1 cup sugar
3 large eggs
1 tablespoon vanilla extract
4 cups all-purpose flour
1 tablespoon baking powder
½ teaspoon baking soda
1 egg white, lightly beaten
Red decorator sugar crystals

Beat butter at medium speed of an electric mixer until creamy; gradually add sugar, beating well. Add eggs and vanilla, beating well. Combine flour, baking powder, and soda; gradually add flour mixture to butter mixture, beating at low speed after each addition just until blended.

Divide dough into fourths. Divide each fourth into 14 portions, and roll each portion into a 9-inch rope. Fold each rope in half, and twist. Shape twists into candy canes; brush with egg white, and sprinkle evenly with sugar crystals.

Place cookies 2 inches apart on ungreased cookie sheets; bake at 350° for 15 to 18 minutes or until edges begin to brown. Remove to wire racks; let cool completely. Yield: 4½ dozen.

"Look at 'em all sitting there; they look familiar, but who the hell are they?"

Bourbon Brownies

1   cup sugar
1   cup butter or margarine
¼   cup water
1   (12-ounce) package semisweet chocolate morsels (2 cups)
½   cup bourbon
2   teaspoons vanilla extract
4   large eggs, lightly beaten
1½ cups all-purpose flour
½   teaspoon baking soda
½   teaspoon salt
2   cups chopped walnuts or pecans
½   cup butter or margarine, softened
2   cups sifted powdered sugar
1   teaspoon vanilla extract
1   (2-ounce) square chocolate-flavored candy coating

Combine first 3 ingredients in a saucepan; bring to a boil. Remove from heat; add morsels and next 2 ingredients, stirring until morsels melt. Gradually stir in eggs. Combine flour, soda, and salt; add to chocolate mixture, mixing well. Stir in nuts. Spoon batter into a greased 15- x 10- x 1-inch jellyroll pan. Bake at 325° for 15 to 20 minutes; cool in pan on a wire rack.

   Combine ½ cup butter, powdered sugar, and 1 teaspoon vanilla; beat at medium speed of an electric mixer until smooth. Spread over brownie layer; cover and chill.

   Place candy coating in a small heavy-duty, zip-top plastic bag. Microwave at MEDIUM (50% power) 2 minutes or until coating melts. Snip a small hole in one corner of bag; drizzle over brownies. Cover and chill until coating hardens. Cut into 2-inch squares. Yield: about 3 dozen.

Festive Fruitcake

¼	cup brandy
1	(6-ounce) can frozen unsweetened orange juice concentrate, thawed and undiluted
1	cup fresh cranberries, chopped
1	(8-ounce) package pitted dates, chopped
1	cup chopped pecans
½	cup egg substitute
1	(8-ounce) can unsweetened pineapple tidbits, drained
1	tablespoon grated orange rind
1	teaspoon vanilla extract
2	cups all-purpose flour
1¼	teaspoons baking soda
¼	teaspoon salt
½	teaspoon ground cinnamon
¼	teaspoon ground nutmeg
¼	teaspoon ground allspice
Vegetable cooking spray	
½	cup brandy
3	tablespoons apple jelly

Combine first 3 ingredients in a large bowl; let stand 1 hour.

Combine dates and next 5 ingredients; stir into cranberry mixture. Combine flour and next 5 ingredients. Stir into fruit mixture. Spoon batter into a 6-cup Bundt or tube pan coated with cooking spray; bake at 325° for 45 minutes or until a wooden pick inserted in center comes out clean. Cool in pan 20 minutes. Remove from pan; cool completely on wire rack.

Bring ½ cup brandy to a boil; cool. Moisten several layers of cheesecloth with brandy, and wrap cake. Cover with plastic wrap; then aluminum foil. Store in a cool place at least 1 week, or freeze up to 3 months. Before serving, melt apple jelly in a saucepan over low heat, stirring constantly; brush over cake. Yield: 21 servings (about 153 calories per slice).

Chocolate Pound Cake

Vegetable cooking spray
1¾ cups sifted cake flour
2 teaspoons baking powder
¼ teaspoon salt
3 tablespoons unsweetened cocoa
¼ teaspoon ground cinnamon
¾ cup sugar
½ cup vegetable oil
½ cup evaporated skim milk
1 tablespoon vanilla extract
4 egg whites, stiffly beaten

Coat bottom of an 8½- x 4½- x 3-inch loafpan with cooking spray; dust lightly with flour, and set aside.

Combine cake flour and next 5 ingredients in a large bowl. Add oil, milk, and vanilla; beat at medium speed of an electric mixer until smooth (batter will be thick). Add one-third of beaten egg whites, and stir gently; fold in remaining whites.

Pour batter into prepared pan. Bake at 350° for 45 minutes or until a wooden pick inserted in center comes out clean. Cool in pan 10 minutes; remove from pan, and cool on a wire rack. Yield: 16 servings (151 calories per ½-inch slice).

Tangy Cranberry Ice

4   cups cranberry juice cocktail
2   teaspoons grated orange rind
2   cups unsweetened orange juice

Combine all ingredients in a 13- x 9- x 2-inch pan; freeze until firm. Remove from freezer, and let stand 15 to 20 minutes. Spoon frozen mixture into a large mixing bowl; beat at low speed of an electric mixer until smooth. Return to freezer until ready to serve. Let stand at room temperature until mixture can be scooped into balls. Serve in individual compotes. Yield: 8 servings (103 calories per 1-cup serving).

Tangy Cranberry Ice, *facing page*

White Lightning Chili, page 94

No End in Sight
✤leftovers✤

Just as you were swearing never to eat or cook again, there are the leftovers. Your mission: to create soups, salads, casseroles, and sandwiches out of these until sometime mid-February. Thank heaven the leftovers, like the family, get even better with the passage of time.

White Lightning Chili

1	pound dried navy beans
4	(14½-ounce) cans ready-to-serve chicken broth, divided
1	large onion, chopped
2	cloves garlic, minced
1	tablespoon ground white pepper
1	tablespoon dried oregano
1	tablespoon ground cumin
½	teaspoon ground cloves
5	cups chopped cooked turkey
2	(4-ounce) cans chopped green chiles, undrained
1	cup water
1	teaspoon salt
1	jalapeño pepper, seeded and chopped

Shredded Monterey Jack cheese
Commercial salsa
Sour cream
Sliced green onions

Sort and wash beans; place in a large Dutch oven. Cover with water 2 inches above beans; let soak 8 hours. Drain beans, and return to pan. Add 3 cans chicken broth, chopped onion, and next 5 ingredients. Bring to a boil; cover, reduce heat, and simmer 2 hours or until beans are tender.

Add remaining can of chicken broth, turkey, and next 4 ingredients. Bring to a boil; cover, reduce heat, and simmer 1 hour, stirring occasionally. Serve with cheese, salsa, sour cream, and green onions. Yield: 2¾ quarts.

Bare Bones Turkey Soup

1	turkey carcass
4	quarts water
1	cup butter or margarine
1	cup all-purpose flour
3	onions, chopped
2	large carrots, diced
2	stalks celery, diced
1	cup long-grain rice, uncooked
2	teaspoons salt
³⁄₄	teaspoon pepper
2	cups half-and-half

Place turkey carcass and water in a large Dutch oven; bring to a boil. Cover, reduce heat, and simmer 1 hour. Remove carcass from broth, and pick meat from bones. Set meat aside. Measure broth; add water to broth, if necessary, to measure 3 quarts. Set aside.

Heat butter in Dutch oven; add flour, and cook over medium heat, stirring constantly, 5 minutes. (Roux will be a very light color.)

Stir onion, carrot, and celery into roux; cook over medium heat 10 minutes, stirring often. Add reserved 3 quarts broth, turkey, rice, salt, and pepper; bring mixture to a boil. Cover, reduce heat, and simmer 20 minutes or until rice is tender. Add half-and-half, and cook until soup is thoroughly heated. Yield: 4½ quarts.

Turkey Parmesan

¼   cup butter or margarine
¼   cup chopped onion
¼   cup chopped celery
¼   cup sliced fresh mushrooms
1   clove garlic, minced
¼   cup all-purpose flour
2   cups milk
2   cups chopped cooked turkey
⅓   cup grated Parmesan cheese
1   tablespoon chopped fresh parsley
1   tablespoon dry white wine
1   teaspoon Worcestershire sauce
¼   teaspoon salt
¼   teaspoon pepper
¼   teaspoon poultry seasoning
3   drops of hot sauce
Pinch of red pepper
Hot cooked noodles

Melt butter in a large heavy skillet. Add onion and next 3 ingredients, and cook over medium heat, stirring constantly, until tender. Add flour, stirring until smooth; cook 1 minute, stirring constantly. Gradually add milk; cook over medium heat, stirring constantly, until thickened and bubbly. Add turkey and next 9 ingredients; stir well, and cook until thoroughly heated. Serve over noodles. Yield: 6 servings.

Stir-Fried Turkey

1   (10-ounce) package frozen Japanese vegetables
2   tablespoons vegetable oil
3   cups cooked turkey strips
1   cup thinly sliced green onions
1   cup thinly sliced celery
½   medium-size green pepper, cut into thin strips
½   medium-size sweet red pepper, cut into thin strips
1   (8-ounce) can sliced water chestnuts, drained
¼   teaspoon ground ginger
⅛   teaspoon crushed red pepper
1   cup water
2   tablespoons soy sauce
1½ tablespoons cornstarch
1   teaspoon teriyaki sauce
Chow mein noodles

Reserve seasoning packet from frozen vegetables for another use. Heat oil in a large skillet. Add frozen vegetables, turkey, and next 7 ingredients; cook over medium-high heat, stirring constantly, until tender. Remove mixture from skillet; set aside.

Combine water, soy sauce, cornstarch, and teriyaki sauce; stir well. Pour mixture into skillet; cook over medium heat, stirring constantly, until mixture boils. Boil 1 minute, stirring constantly, until mixture is smooth and thickened. Remove from heat; add turkey mixture, stirring gently. Serve over chow mein noodles. Yield: 6 servings.

Ham Loaf from Heaven

1	pound ground cooked ham
1	pound ground fresh pork
2	large eggs, lightly beaten
½	teaspoon onion powder
¼	teaspoon salt
¼	teaspoon seasoned pepper
1	cup cracker crumbs
¾	cup firmly packed brown sugar
1½	teaspoons dry mustard
¼	cup white vinegar
1	(16-ounce) can whole-berry cranberry sauce

Combine first 7 ingredients. Shape mixture into a 9- x 5-inch loaf; place in a lightly greased 10- x 6- x 2-inch baking dish. Combine sugar, mustard, and vinegar; spoon half of sugar mixture over ham loaf. Bake at 350° for 1 hour and 20 minutes, basting twice with remaining sugar mixture. Top with cranberry sauce, and bake 10 additional minutes. Yield: 6 to 8 servings.

"Sometimes we all just need a little privacy, that's all. Some time to breathe on our own."

Ham and Cheese Dagwood Sandwich

1   (1-pound) round loaf sourdough bread
½   cup mayonnaise or salad dressing
2½ teaspoons dried Italian seasoning
½   teaspoon pepper
1   large onion, thinly sliced
2   medium-size green or sweet red peppers, cut into thin strips
1   stalk celery, sliced
1   tablespoon olive oil
1   pound cooked ham, thinly sliced (about 25 slices)
1½ cups (6 ounces) shredded Cheddar and mozzarella cheese
       blend

Slice off top third of bread loaf; set top aside. Hollow out bottom section, leaving a ½-inch shell. (Reserve crumbs for another use.)

Combine mayonnaise, Italian seasoning, and pepper. Brush inside of bread shell with half of mayonnaise mixture. Set shell and remaining mixture aside.

Cook onion, pepper strips, and celery in olive oil in a large skillet over medium-high heat, stirring constantly, until tender.

Arrange half of ham in bread shell, and top with half of vegetable mixture; sprinkle with half of cheese. Spread remaining mayonnaise mixture over cheese. Repeat layers with remaining ham, vegetable mixture, and cheese. Replace bread top. Wrap sandwich in heavy-duty aluminum foil.

Bake at 400° for 30 minutes or until thoroughly heated. Cut sandwich into wedges, and serve immediately. Yield: 6 servings.

Ham and Broccoli Strata

12   slices white bread, crusts removed
1   (10-ounce) package frozen chopped broccoli, cooked and
        drained
2   cups diced cooked ham
6   large eggs, lightly beaten
3   cups (12 ounces) shredded sharp Cheddar cheese
3½ cups milk
1   tablespoon dried onion flakes
¼   teaspoon dry mustard
Garnish: parsley sprigs

Cut bread into small cubes. Layer cubes, broccoli, and ham
in a lightly greased 13- x 9- x 2-inch baking dish.
    Combine eggs and next 4 ingredients; stir well. Pour
over casserole; cover and refrigerate up to 24 hours. Bake,
uncovered, at 325° for 50 to 55 minutes. Garnish, if desired.
Yield: 6 to 8 servings.

Turkey-Wild Rice Casserole

3   cups canned low-sodium chicken broth, undiluted
3   cups sliced fresh mushrooms
6   ounces wild rice, uncooked
3   cups chopped cooked turkey breast (skinned before
       cooking and cooked without fat)
²/₃ cup oil-free Italian dressing
1   cup low-fat sour cream
Vegetable cooking spray

Bring chicken broth to a boil in medium saucepan; stir in mushrooms. Reduce heat; simmer 5 minutes. Remove mushrooms with a slotted spoon, and set aside. Add rice to broth; stir well. Cover and cook 1 hour and 5 minutes or until liquid is absorbed.

Combine rice, reserved mushrooms, turkey, dressing, and sour cream; spoon into a 2-quart baking dish coated with cooking spray. Bake, uncovered, at 325° for 45 minutes. Let stand 10 minutes before serving. Yield: 6 servings (298 calories per serving).

"Nobody means what they say on Thanksgiving, you know that."

Turkey Fried Rice

1¼ cups water
1½ cups instant brown rice, uncooked
2 tablespoons reduced-calorie margarine
2 tablespoons low-sodium soy sauce
2 cups chopped cooked turkey
½ cup frozen English peas
½ cup coarsely shredded carrot
¼ cup thinly sliced green onions
¼ cup coarsely chopped green pepper
1 large egg, lightly beaten

Bring water to a boil in a saucepan; stir in rice. Cook rice according to package directions, omitting salt and fat. Cover and set aside.

Melt margarine in a large saucepan over low heat; stir in soy sauce. Add turkey; cover and cook 5 minutes. Add peas and next 3 ingredients; cook 3 minutes over medium heat, stirring constantly. Stir in egg, and cook 1 minute or until egg is done, stirring constantly.

Combine rice and turkey mixture; stir well. Serve warm. Yield: 5 servings (about 258 calories per 1-cup serving).

Turkey of a Salad

4½   cups loosely packed torn romaine lettuce
1½   cups loosely packed torn radicchio
1½   cups cubed cooked turkey
¼   cup vertically sliced purple onion
1   (11-ounce) can mandarin oranges in lite syrup, drained
¼   cup unsweetened orange juice
1½   tablespoons red wine vinegar
1½   teaspoons poppy seeds
1½   teaspoons olive oil
¼   teaspoon Dijon mustard
⅛   teaspoon salt
⅛   teaspoon pepper

Combine first 5 ingredients in a bowl. Combine orange juice
and remaining ingredients in a bowl; stir well. Pour over salad,
tossing gently to coat. Serve immediately. Yield: 4 servings
(about 166 calories per 2-cup serving).

Melting Pot Sandwiches

6	canned medium-size mild Greek peppers
6	large, thin onion slices, separated into rings
3	tablespoons oil-free Italian dressing
1	tablespoon plus 1 teaspoon prepared mustard
4	(2-ounce) whole wheat French bread rolls, split lengthwise
8	ounces thinly sliced cooked roast beef
2	ounces provolone cheese, cut into thin strips

Remove and discard stems from peppers. Cut peppers into ¼-inch slices; set aside.

Combine onion and Italian dressing in a small saucepan; bring to a boil. Reduce heat, and simmer just until onion is transparent. Set mixture aside. (Do not drain.)

Spread 1 teaspoon mustard on bottom half of each roll; top each with 2 ounces roast beef. Spoon reserved onion mixture evenly over sandwiches; top with pepper slices and cheese. Top with remaining halves of rolls. Wrap each sandwich individually in aluminum foil. Bake at 350° for 10 minutes or until sandwiches are thoroughly heated. Serve warm. Yield: 4 servings (347 calories per serving).

Topless Pork Sandwiches

2   tablespoons plain nonfat yogurt
1   tablespoon commercial mango chutney
¼   cup shredded lettuce
2   (1-ounce) slices pumpernickel bread, toasted
8   thin unpeeled pear slices
4   (½-ounce) slices Apple-Glazed Pork Roast, halved
        lengthwise (page 33)
2   tablespoons Brie cheese

Combine yogurt and chutney; stir well, and set aside.

Place half of shredded lettuce on each slice of pumpernickel bread; drizzle 1½ tablespoons yogurt mixture over lettuce. Alternate pear slices and pork slices over each. Top each with 1 tablespoon cheese. Broil 5½ inches from heat 2 minutes or until cheese melts. Serve immediately. Yield: 2 servings (about 242 calories per serving).

"What the hell does Dear Abby know about life anyway?"

☙Metric Measure Conversions☙

When You Know...	Multiply by... Mass (weight)	To Find Approximate...	Symbol
ounces	28	grams	g
pounds	0.45	kilograms	kg
	(volume)		
teaspoons	5	milliliters	ml
tablespoons	15	milliliters	ml
fluid ounces	30	milliliters	ml
cups	0.24	liters	l
pints	0.47	liters	l
quarts	0.95	liters	l
gallons	3.8	liters	l

☙Metric Measure Equivalents☙

Cup Measure	Volume (Liquid)	Solid (Butter)	Fine Powder (Flour)	Granular (Sugar)	Grain (Rice)
1	250 ml	200 g	140 g	190 g	150 g
3/4	188 ml	150 g	105 g	143 g	113 g
2/3	167 ml	133 g	93 g	127 g	100 g
1/2	125 ml	100 g	70 g	95 g	75 g
1/3	83 ml	67 g	47 g	63 g	50 g
1/4	63 ml	50 g	35 g	48 g	38 g
1/8	31 ml	25 g	18 g	24 g	19 g

☩ Index ☩

Photography by Ralph Anderson, Sylvia Martin, Howard S. Puckett, and Charles Walton IV.
Photo styling by Cindy Manning Barr, Virginia R. Cravens, and Leslie Byars Simpson.

Thanks also to Steve Bender, the big cut-up behind the turkey carving directions on page 36.